"No one can find a full life without feeling understood at least by one person. Misunderstood, he loses his self-confidence, he loses his faith in life, or even in God."

PAUL TOURNIER is a Swiss physician who has made a significant contribution to our understanding of psychiatry and its relation to the Christian faith. Among his other books are *The Meaning of Gifts, Secrets, The Seasons of Life,* and *To Resist or To Surrender?*

To Understand Each Other

Paul Tournier

TRANSLATED BY JOHN S. GILMOUR

A JOVE BOOK

150.19
TOT

This is a translation of *Difficultés conjugales,* published by
Editions Labor et Fides, Geneva, Switzerland, 1962.

This Jove book contains the complete
text of the original hardcover edition.
It has been completely reset in a typeface
designed for easy reading, and was printed
from new film.

TO UNDERSTAND EACH OTHER

A Jove book / published by arrangement with
John Knox Press

PRINTING HISTORY
Two previous printings
John Knox Press edition published 1967
Jove edition / January 1978
Third printing / June 1982

ISBN: 0-515-06417-3

Library of Congress Catalog Card Number: 67-15298

Jove books are published by Jove Publications, Inc.,
200 Madison Avenue, New York, N. Y. 10016.
The words "A JOVE BOOK" and the "J" with sunburst
are trademarks belonging to Jove Publications, Inc.
PRINTED IN THE UNITED STATES OF AMERICA

Contents

To Understand Each Other

To Achieve Understanding, We Need to Want It

A few days ago I was introduced to an American colleague, a surgeon from New York. He immediately impressed me as most likable. Yet, we had quite a problem in understanding each other, because I speak only a few words in English, and he but a few words in French! Even so, we managed to get through to one another, for both of us most ardently wanted to. This remark brings us fully into the subject matter of our study.

We must be reminded that the first condition for mutual understanding is the desire for, the seeking after, and the willing of that understanding. Such a statement may appear very commonplace. Nevertheless, this basic attitude toward understanding others is far rarer than we think. Listen to all the conversations of our world, those between nations as well as those between couples. They are for the most part dialogues of the deaf. Each one speaks primarily in

order to set forth his own ideas, in order to justify himself, in order to enhance himself and to accuse others. Exceedingly few exchanges of viewpoints manifest a real desire to understand the other person.

My surgeon friend was completely taken up with his work in a New York hospital. His interesting career and brilliant success brought him a feeling of full satisfaction. There was only one thing wrong: his wife was very nervous. He sent her, therefore, to a friend, one of New York's thousands of psychiatrists. Since his mother also was nervous, he sent her to a second psychiatrist. Then he sent his mother-in-law to a third. Thus he had fulfilled his duty. Surgeons, after all, make no pretense of knowing about psychological matters. For these they refer their clients to a specialist.

One day, the psychiatrist who was treating his wife had him come and told him, "You know, you are not giving enough attention to your wife. You should take her out to a show at least once a week." Now the surgeon was not lacking in goodwill; he was quite ready to follow the psychiatrist's counsel. "It is agreed," he soon replied; "I'll take my wife out to the movies every Friday evening." And he did just that. He confessed to me how good he felt in his conscience when they used to come home from the show. Now that his wife had had her outing with him, she could no longer complain of his leaving her alone, because of his work, the rest of the week.

We can see how judicious was the psychiatrist's counsel. He saw very clearly that basically the wife was suffering because her husband did not pay enough attention to her. This couple was one of many such where gradually man and wife had grown apart without there ever having taken place any serious conflict. That is why I choose this example. When we talk of "marriage counseling" we think immediately of the extreme cases, of threats to seek divorce, of couples in violent disputes who frequently come to blows. But there are many others which deserve our attention and care because their marriage is no less a failure: they live side by side, without hurting one another, but poles apart because of no real understanding of one another.

Now our surgeon, after the help given by his psychiatrist friend, understood that his wife needed to go out with her husband to the show at least once a week. It was a step in the right direction. Basically, however, he still had not understood his wife. There is an important difference between degrees of understanding. Many people live for years together without deep understanding, without even seeking it. This we see in outstanding, cultured, intelligent families, people of the very highest order, learned men, even professors of psychology. They appear unaware of something that is missing in their life, wonderful as it may be in other ways. Their home life has not remained a living reality. If they feel some vague pangs of conscience about it, they can soothe these by taking the wife out to the show on Friday night.

Most couples enter into conjugal life with a high ideal for marriage. Some even have taken courses for engaged couples, have read thick and learned books on sexual life. They have learned many interesting things, studied works on psychology, sometimes even too much so! How many of them can say, a dozen years later, that their home has become what they expected of it? All too few! This is the problem we are confronting and about which we shall be thinking.

Every man whose hopes are not fulfilled is naturally inclined toward blaming others for his setback: it's the other fellow's fault! It is much easier than seeking out the inner fault, but it is absolutely sterile. This road leads only to spite, bitterness, inner revolt, and the stereotyped mutual recriminations that marital partners continually make. Or else they blame

fate. The man thinks that his bad fortune was to "chance" upon such an impossible woman. His wife blames fate for a man who is insupportable.

In order to escape his responsibility, each is inclined to accuse the character of his partner, her bad health, her faults, her upbringing, or the influence of the altogether different environment in which she was raised. Now such matters are very important. We must seek to guide our children in the choice of a fiancé or fiancée. A certain degree of common background is useful. But it would be sheer folly to think that marital success and the possibility of full understanding of one another depends primarily upon one's background. No, for marriage is above all what we make of it from day to day. "It is a work of art," as Dr. Lucien Bovet used to say.

Let us react then against the stupid idea of chance which leads men to imagine that we may hit upon "a pearl" for a wife as one might a prize in a lottery. Besides, it could be very difficult to be married to "a pearl" if you did not feel yourself in the same category!

What really counts, then, is the working out together of marital happiness. It is a goal to strive after, not a privilege gained at the outset. And to work it out, the ability to understand each other is essential. So-called emotional incompatibility is a myth invented by jurists short of arguments in order to plead for divorce. It is likewise a common excuse people use in order to hide their own failings. I simply do not believe it exists. There are no emotional incompatibilities. There are misunderstandings and mistakes, however, which can be corrected where there is the willingness to do so.

The most frequent fault seems to me to be the lack of complete frankness. I see many couples. Behind their difficulties I always discover this lack of mutual openness, a loyal and total openness to one another without which there can be no real understanding. A couple who are courageous enough always to say everything will without a doubt go through many upsets, but they will be able to build an ever more successful marriage. On the other hand, all dissimulating becomes only the portent, and the way toward, failure.

Many couples no longer realize that they are hiding a part of their real feelings from each other, a part of their ideas, convictions, and personal reactions. Upon entering my office one husband told me quite sincerely, "I certainly talk everything over with my wife." Afterward, we talked together about many things which interest him vitally. Then I asked him, "What does your wife think of all that?" "Oh," was the blurted-out reply, "I would never mention these to her; she wouldn't understand."

"She wouldn't understand." In other words, she wouldn't share my opinions, and I want to avoid any argument. Thus it is that in order to have peace many couples put aside certain subjects—those that are emotionally charged—those that are most important for their coming to a true mutual understanding. Thus, bit by bit, the transparent window which the relationship between man and wife should be becomes blurred. They are starting to become strangers to one another. They are losing the total oneness which is the divine law for marriage.

When instituting marriage, God declared, "They shall no longer be two, but one." To be one obviously means not to have secrets from each other. As soon as a couple begin to hide matters from one another they compromise the basic oneness of marital life. They start off on the road to failure. This is true even if it is done out of the best intentions, or even if it is a very good thing that is hidden. (We can hide just as easily our subjects of pride as those of shame.) We may try to patch things up, start over again, attempt a reconciliation. But a real rebirth will always have as its condition a far deeper and more difficult mutual frankness.

My Husband Is a Mysterious Island!

For many couples it is almost with pain that they recall the days of courtship. At that time they appeared to understand each other! Why is that? Because they talked to each other, they opened up to one another, they found great pleasure in understanding and in being understood. The frankness of one evoked the openness of the other. The man was discovering the real person of his fiancée. She felt understood by him, and he by her.

Now they no longer really talk to each other. Oh, they talk about many secondary matters, trivial and external to themselves, but the matters that are really essential, intimate, personal—these they no longer mention. The dialogue has been broken off. There is only a superficial exchange of information.

Some couples no longer talk together at all. I have known some who could go for weeks without saying a word! It engenders a horrible atmosphere in the home. Just think how children must grow up where at the meal table one of the parents never speaks, whereas the other, in an attempt to fill the atrocious vacuum, never ceases babbling on!

Courtship's beautiful curiosity has been lost. The thirst for discovery and for understanding has been dried up. The husband believes that now he does understand his wife. At the first word from her lips he makes a little sign of exasperation which means, "You're still telling me the same old story!" In the face of such a reaction how can the other dare to express herself? Yet, the less she expresses herself, the less she will be understood; the less she feels understood, the more she will withdraw into herself. The thrill of discovery has been lost. If you think that you know your wife or your husband, it is because you have given up the real attempt to discover him. The difference between the image you have made of him, and what he really is, will ever grow deeper.

The discovery of the real person is never easy. I remember a woman who had come to speak to me of her very serious worries. At the end of our interview I asked her, "What does your husband think of all that?" "Oh," she blurted out, "my husband is a mysterious island. I am forever circling around it but never finding a beach where I may land." I understood her, for it is true. There are men who are like mysterious islands. They protect themselves against any approach. They no longer express themselves, nor do they take a stand on anything. When their wife consults them on something important, they hide themselves behind their paper. They look deeply absorbed. They answer without even looking up, in a tone impersonal, anonymous, and vague, which excludes all argument. Or else they escape by making a joke of it.

To Achieve Understanding,
We Need to Express Ourselves

If the first condition for the achievement of understanding is the will to understand, the second condition is that of expressing oneself. Every human being needs to express himself. Through lack of opportunity for it, one may become sick. Of course it is not only in marriage that we can express ourselves. There are also all those relationships with others in our social world: friends, brothers and sisters, relatives, and so on. However, if a person is married, it is toward his wife that his need to express himself is the greatest. There are men who complain of the poor health of their wives without realizing that the latter are sick simply because their husbands never listen to them. In order to express oneself, there must be a feeling of warm and kind receptivity and of attentive listening.

Each of us easily finds cause for avoiding real encounter. One wife told me, "When I start to speak to my husband about important matters, he puts on his hat and goes out; he heads off to his lodge." Another wife, however, may well interrupt an important conversation in order to go take care of useful matters, but matters which could well be looked after when her husband is at the office. We can easily find duties in order to escape face-to-face relationships. The fact is that many married people flee from it; they are afraid of opening up in depth. They do not take the time which is necessary for it. Even when on vacation they run about seeking every kind of distraction, invite home very charming friends, friends who enable them to avoid calm and peaceful talk together. A great deal of time must be taken in order to build a true marriage, a great deal more than my American colleague's Friday evenings. A deep encounter rarely takes place in a few moments. It must be prepared for by hours of careful drawing together.

To Àchieve Understánding, We Need Courage

This affirmation will doubtless astonish many readers who imagine that we can open ourselves to others quite easily. Up to a certain point, yes we can, but not completely. Some jovial and sociable people flatter themselves that they are able easily to open up, but the truth is, it is but a superficial opening up. Actually, beneath their flow of words their deepest thoughts and feelings lie hidden, just as withdrawn people hide theirs by their silence. A complete unveiling of one's inner thoughts, an absolute necessity for real and deep understanding, demands a great deal of courage. I was listening for some time to a woman who was telling me about her husband; speaking about him, in fact, much more than about herself. "Really," I said to her, "You are afraid of your husband." Our contact was strong enough for her to answer me honestly, "Yes, I am afraid of my husband."

Let us not suppose for a moment that wives are alone in being afraid. Husbands too are afraid of their wives. Men are more proud than women and have greater difficulty in admitting their being afraid. This is one of the differences between men and women: women often display their fears quite openly while men hide theirs. A man will hide them, for example, by means of his authoritarian manner. By one word, harsh and cutting, he stops his wife's talking and puts an end to the conversation which he fears. Or else he gives grandiose intellectual and scientific explanations which save him from any personal commitment. He wants to have the last word always, and veils through his over-talking his fear of being contradicted. Perhaps the same end is achieved through a display of anger or, again, through obstinate silence.

What is this fear? I believe there are two parts to it. First, there is the fear of being judged, the fear of criticism. This is universal fear, and far greater than we generally suppose. Moreover, it is from our wife, or our best friend, from the very people that we admire and love the most, that we fear critical judgment the most. This is precisely because their admiration and love mean so much to us.

Now, all of us judge ourselves. We well know that if we want to be completely honest and be seen as we really are, stripped of the attractive character which we are ceaselessly trying to play in life, we shall have to speak of things about which we are ashamed. It is, after all, those nearest to us who best know our weaknesses, who with full reason can reproach us for them. This is why so many couples play at hide-and-go-seek. They fear that conversation, by becoming more real, will open wounds to which they are most sensitive, wounds made all the more painful because they are inflicted by one's closest partner.

It is true that many couples are quick in judging one another. One judgment responds to another in a sort of vicious and diabolical circle. Each, in order to protect his failings from the other, denounces the other's shortcomings, either inwardly or quite out loud. Few people really accept the fact that their marital partner behaves in a profoundly different way from themselves Yet how often you hear them say, "I cannot understand my husband" or "I cannot understand my wife."

Here is a wife, a little too suspicious; she sometimes opens letters addressed to her husband. The latter tells me, "I just cannot understand such lack of respect." What would be important to understand is the origin of this mistrustful trait and what brought about its accentuation later on. Here is a father who insists that his son become an engineer. "This child is wasting his time," says the mother; "he has no bent toward such studies. His love is for music, even jazz. It is beyond reason; I cannot understand my husband." It would be important to know precisely what events in the father's personal life have put such an obstinate desire in his heart to make an engineer out of his son

"I cannot understand my wife," a husband says; "she complains of fatigue and yet in the evening she can never decide to go to bed. She runs around doing a thousand useless things. It's useless for me to tell her to go to bed. Nothing doing. It is both stupid and irritating." It would be important to know what makes her so nervously active in the evening. Here is a wife who complains, "I cannot understand why my husband finds it so hard to get up in the morning. I have to call him again and again. Then, when he does arise, he has no time for breakfast and he arrives late at his office. He will end up by losing his job. It is senseless." What would be most interesting to know is why this man finds getting up so difficult. He probably doesn't know the reason himself. What he does know is that his mother scolded him for the same thing years ago, and that all his resolutions to improve have remained unfulfilled.

The "I cannot understand" really means "I cannot understand that my husband is different from me, that he thinks, feels, and acts in a quite different manner than I." So the husband feels judged, condemned, criticized. All of us fear this, for no one is satisfied with himself. We are especially sensitive to blame for shortcomings which we ourselves find stupid, and which we have never been able to correct in spite of our sincerest efforts.

There is a second fear, that of receiving advice. Let us take the example of a husband who is having trouble at the office. At first he mentions this to his wife, but she, carried away by a zeal to come to his aid, replies too readily, "You absolutely must get rid of that ineffective associate. Stand up for yourself, or he'll walk right over you! How many times have I told you already you're too weak! Go and report this to the management . . ." In other words, a shower of inapplicable counsels. This woman does not realize the complexity of the problems which her husband must face up to. And he, he feels that she holds him responsible for all his problems, and treats him like a little boy.

The husband began by unveiling his anxieties, but, in the face of such ready-made answers, he withdraws. He is crushed in his hope before being able to show his wife all the aspects of a delicate problem. The wife's intention was excellent, but she ruined everything by replying too quickly. She should have listened longer and tried to understand.

It is tragic because the wife tried to help her husband. One of the highest functions of a wife is to console her husband for all the blows he receives in life. Yet, in order to console, there is no need to say very much. It is enough to listen, to understand, to love. Look at that mother whose child runs crying to her knees. She utters no word, and yet in a moment the tears have disappeared, the child jumps down, smiles all over his face, and heads out into the world once more where he will receive new blows. In every man, even the most eminent and the apparently strongest, there remains something of the child who needs to be consoled.

Ten years from now the wife of whom we've been speaking may come to my office and tell me, "Whenever we have visitors, my husband talks a great deal about his business. This is the only way I can learn anything about it. Yet, I should so much like to understand his work. Whenever we are alone, he says nothing. I sense that he is seriously preoccupied, I ask him to tell me of his work, but he says that I could never understand such matters." This woman does not realize that she herself has paralyzed her husband's ability to unburden his heart.

People are always much more sensitive than we believe them to be. Often men are just as easily hurt as women, even though they hide it. They are afraid of being hurt by advice just as much as by criticism. They resent it every bit as much. A woman for whom everything seems clear-cut, who confidently tells her husband how he must act in order to do the right thing, no matter what the problem may be—such a woman gives her husband the impression that she thinks him incompetent. No husband can put up with this.

Naturally, the reverse is just as true of the husband who replies too readily to the problems his wife confides to him, and who wants to give her good advice. She may be in conflict with a neighbor who gives hurting looks or also utters cutting words to her in the elevator. "Don't take it seriously," he quickly replies; "of what importance is all that? You are too sensitive!" The wife then feels misunderstood by her husband. She even feels that he sides with the neighbor—instead of sticking up for her. Thus she becomes in fact ever more sensitive to daily affronts. Nor can she any longer feel free to unburden herself by talking about it to her husband.

In order really to understand, we need to listen, not to reply. We need to listen long and attentively. In order to help anybody to open his heart, we have to give him time, asking only a few questions, as carefully as possible, in order to help him better explain his experience. Above all we must not give the impression that we know better than he does what he must do. Otherwise we force him to withdraw. Too much criticism will also achieve the same result, so fragile are his inner sensitivities.

There are also husbands who say, "I do not want to burden my wife with worry; I keep my problems to myself." These husbands may be sincere in thinking thus, but they are deluding themselves. There are always deeper reasons for such inner blockage of confidences. In any case it is a sign that the marital sharing has failed. A woman can bear any anxiety when she feels supported by her husband, and meets every blow head on, along with him. The worst worry for a woman is perhaps that of feeling that her husband is weighed down with problems which he does not share with her. There are many misunderstood people in this world. But when we look at them close up, we realize that they are always at least partly responsible themselves. If they are not understood, it is because they have not opened up.

Why, then, is it that so many people in my office say to me, "With you I can open up, because you understand"? The truth is rather the reverse; I understand them because they open up. Sometimes I understand them much better than their partners, because they tell me everything they hold back from them. A doctor is also more neutral. His whole career increasingly strips him of the desire to judge and persuades him that one hardly helps with advice unless the one to whom it is given is ready to act on it. And then, a doctor knows nothing yet about his client; he learns all directly from the latter's very lips. Of course he is not fooled by the client's way of presenting matters in his best personal light, but even this is authentic evidence. What counts in life is not so much the facts, but the manner in which we see and interpret them.

Those near to him have already their preconceived image of the person speaking, and this image is always to some extent false, and to some extent falsifies the meaning of what he has to say. This is so true that when we have a client too long in therapy, the time comes when our opinion of him dries up, unknown to us, his readiness to share confidences. He will no longer tell us anything but what he believes we can understand. Once again the fear of being misunderstood has made its appearance in him. We must shed the image which we have conceived of him in order for him to find again all his ease in opening his heart, just as if he were seeing us for the first time.

The same is true between man and wife. Each has a certain image of the other, partially right, but just as surely partially wrong. In any case it is too rigid, an imaginary view, an idea more or less forced by the other, a sort of diagnostic superimposed upon him. It is well known that the most frequent cause of errors in medical diagnosis is the overconfidence of the physician in himself. The diagnosis which he has superimposed upon the patient makes him impervious to every other interpretation of the symptoms.

As soon as a husband feels that his wife has superimposed her moral diagnosis upon him, from which nothing can budge her, all true openess, all deep expression of himself, dries up. It may then happen that this husband will begin to speak with some girl whom he meets at the office or the sports club. He will open up easily to her about many things which he no longer dares to tell his wife. He will rediscover then the wonderful feeling for which every human being hungers, that of being understood. He will perhaps even speak to her of his marital problems. Men easily soften a woman's heart by means of their marriage disappointments. In my office this husband will possibly say, "I cannot live without that young woman. She understands me, while my wife does not." Tragedy is fast approaching!

To Achieve Understanding,
We Need to Love

It is quite clear that between love and understanding there is a very close link. It is so close that we never know where the one ends and the other begins, nor which of the two is the cause or the effect. He who loves understands, and he who understands loves. One who feels understood feels loved, and one who feels loved feels sure of being understood.

A man needs to feel very deeply loved in order to share an intimate secret charged with emotion. Thus he may relate a strange experience which happened one day, and which was for him a mysterious intervention of God in his life. He may tell of some dreamlike ideal to which he holds very deeply. Again, he may tell of an inner call, a sense of mission

which he is to fulfill in this world. It seemed to him that he could never dare speak of it to another. He feared that it would appear ridiculous or vain. And yet, suddenly, without his knowing why, the rapport with another has become such that he uncovers his long-hidden secret.

Deep sharing is overwhelming, and very rare. A thousand fears keep us in check. First of all there is the fear of breaking down, of crying. There is especially the fear that the other will not sense the tremendous importance with which this memory or feeling is charged. How painful it is when such a difficult sharing falls flat, upon ears either preoccupied or mocking, ears in any case that do not sense the significance of what we're saying.

It may happen between man and wife. The partner who has thus spoken in a very personal way without being understood falls back into a terrible emotional solitude. He may become sick because of it. In such circumstances some will go to see their pastor or priest, others their doctor. They are simply seeking someone who can understand. In certain cases of therapy, the help of a doctor or of a man of God may be necessary. Often, however, a wife can bring the same help to her husband, or he to her, if the same painstaking care is exercised in listening as would be done by a pastor, priest, psychologist, or doctor.

How beautiful, how grand and liberating this experience is, when couples learn so to help each other. It is impossible to overemphasize the immense need men have to be really listened to, to be taken seriously, to be understood. The churches have always known this; modern psychology has brought it very much to our attention. At the very heart of all psychotherapy is this type of relationship in which one can tell everything just as a little child may tell all to his mother. No one can develop freely in this world and find a full life without feeling understood by at least one person. Misunderstood, he loses his self-confidence, he loses his faith in life or even in God. He is blocked and he regresses.

Here is an even greater mystery: no one comes to know himself through introspection, or in the solitude of his personal diary. Rather, it is in dialogue, in his meeting with other persons. It is only by expressing his convictions to others that he becomes really conscious of them. He who would see himself clearly must open up to a confidant freely chosen and worthy of such trust. It may be a friend just as easily as a doctor; it may also be one's marital partner.

Marriage then becomes a great adventure, a continuous discovery both of oneself and of one's mate. It becomes a daily broadening of one's horizon, an opportunity of learning something new about life, about human existence, about God. This is why in the beginning of the Bible God says, "It is not good that man should be alone." Man here means the human being: "It is not good that the human being should be alone." The human being needs fellowship; he needs a partner, a real encounter with others. He needs to understand others, and to sense that others understand him.

Such is the very intention of God in instituting marriage, according to the Bible. Alone, a man marks time and becomes very set in his ways. In the demanding confrontation which marriage constitutes, he must ever go beyond himself, develop, grow up into maturity. When marriage is reduced to mere symbiosis of two persons essentially hidden from one another, peaceful though such life may sometimes be, it has completely missed its goal. Then it is not solely the marriage which has failed, but both husband and wife. They have failed in their calling as a man and a woman. To fail to understand one's spouse is to fail to understand oneself. It is also a failure to grow and to fulfill one's possibilities.

Psychologists specializing in marriage relationships have enlightened us a great deal at this point. They speak of three different phases. The first is the "honeymoon phase." The couple feel that they understand each other both easily and amazingly well. You can hear the fiancée saying, "My fiancé has the same taste as I in everything; we're the very same; we agree in all matters and we are able to talk everything over between us. Even before I begin to say something, he has already thought the same. He senses all my wishes and all my feelings he understands."

During the early years of marriage we are still in the honeymoon phase, still have the sense of spontaneous mutual understanding and complete sameness. By instinct, we choose partners complementary to ourselves. What each one has repressed in himself during the period of adolescent differentiation he rediscovers in his partner. Hence the wonderful feeling of completeness in each other.

Then comes the second phase in marriage, usually

found between the fifth and tenth years of marriage, according to the same specialists. In this stage each one realizes that the other is not so similar to himself as he had thought. He discovers faults heretofore unnoticed or else faults which he was sure would disappear quickly under the happy effects of marriage. Now these faults are often of the most insupportable and tanacious kind! They include temper, selfishness, lying, greed, violence, vulgarity, drunkenness. What a letdown! We begin gently by warning the other, then by scolding, by imploring, and finally by threatening. Yet none of these takes effect. Then comes the well-known expression: "I cannot understand him . . ." Then comes the temptation to withdraw into oneself in order to lessen the risk of conflict, the temptation to abdicate.

This is the beginning of the third phase. It will develop according to the direction which the previous phase has taken. It may be the progressive giving up in the struggle for happiness: resentment, bitterness, rebellion. "My husband is not the man I believed he was . . ." "My wife is not at all what I thought her to be . . ." "I made a terrible mistake . . ." At this point they may begin to think of divorce. Or else, they may live an existence of endless disputing, never settled. Again, they may work out a form of agreement by the capitulation of one of the partners to the other who thus gives up his own personality. Or they may yet work out agreement on a much inferior level, throwing the axe handle after the axe. Each will withdraw from the other, organizing his own life and becoming more and more secretive.

The second direction is that of courage. This means the courageous acceptance of reality: taking one's partner such as he is, divested of the flattering halo which we had put over him. It means a real attempt undertaken to understand this so-far-from-attractive partner. Indeed, he has faults; he has problems which he has not succeeded in solving. He does not understand himself and he reacts most distastefully when his faults are pointed out. He reacts in this way precisely because he does not feel capable of overcoming his faults. But he can be helped in a quite different fashion: simply by loving him, not so much for his qualities as for his problems. He can be helped simply by understanding him, understanding what he missed in his childhood years and what he is still missing, and by seeking to fill that need.

Thus it is a matter of facing up to our problems rather than avoiding them, of tackling them together and seeking together their solution by a more penetrating understanding both of self and of one's partner. Problems? There are problems in every marriage! Dr. Weatherhead, the well-known British minister and psychologist, writes in one of his books of a couple who came one evening to tell him, "Oh, us! We've never had an argument." Weatherhead adds that he thought to himself, "Either these people are lying or else one of them has crushed the other."

At the time of engagement it is virtually impossible to imagine these problems. Once I was asked to speak on marital conflict as part of a course given to engaged couples. All of my auditors were fully persuaded that they would never face such conflict. This is the reason why the disappointment is so great when difficulties arise, why there is so much self-pity, why there is the naïve but sincere belief that it is all due to an exceptional misfortune.

The couple is greatly relieved just to hear us say, "You have problems? That's quite normal; all couples do. As a matter of fact it is a good thing. Those who make a success of their marriage are those who tackle their problems together and who overcome them. Those who lack the courage to do this are the ones whose marriage is a failure." Such a couple is helped even more by telling them of our own difficulties, of the problems which had to be worked out in our marriage, of the time we had to take in order to understand each other better, of the crises which were necessary, and of the profound changes through which we had to go in order to achieve a oneness more real and more respectful of our differences.

Yes, it is the very differences in our characters, tastes, habits, prejudices, and convictions which oblige us to a greater effort to understand each other. These in turn lead to further growth in both of us. I found a fine reference to this by Madame Tolstoy, wife of the famous writer, in her personal diary: "I write in my diary only when we are angry with each other." That is, conflict with her husband gave her a healthy shaking up, awoke in her many thoughts which she worked out in her diary. Of course, the following day when they were together, all that must have seemed far less important than what she had thought it to be.

Yet, there is always an element of truth in these

emotional moments aroused by a crisis. It is the following day that it is important to examine, calmly and together, the latent problems revealed by the crisis. That is the time that a greater mutual unveiling will give them new light by which the hidden causes will be seen. Many couples, however, once they've happily regained aimiability, turn over a new leaf, as they say, without having learned anything from the crisis. They put off their real encounter until the next crisis renews it in its violent and fruitless form.

It takes courage to face up to all the problems created by a complete adaptation of two personalities. People are very different one from another. This is a fact plain to see; yet, few will admit it, especially when it is a question of their wife or their husband. That he should have other tastes, other feelings, and other hopes is immediately reacted to as a challenge, a defiance, an attack, a rejection. We see this same reaction in parents when they discover in their adolescent children tendencies which they highly disdain. To come to understand that one's partner is very different—this already presupposes a great deal of personal growth.

To Achieve Understanding,
We Need to Accept Our Natural Differences

I am thinking of some friends. The husband is a university professor and a renowned author. Now thinkers and poets need long moments of quietness for meditation, moments in which they apparently do nothing, but which in reality permit their thoughts to take clear expression. "Since you're not doing anything," interrupts the wife, a very busy housekeeper, "come and help me put up the ladder in our garden to pick some apples." Since you're not doing anything! Here we have the conflict of two temperaments, the one meditative, the other activist. Our professor friend feels himself not understood. Another man's wife fails to understand that her husband needs to work with his hands after a day in the office. If he takes up a saw, she sees only the cleaning up of the rug which she will have to do, and she objects. Yet, her husband could take certain precautions. He has not yet understood how his wife identifies herself with her home, to the point that if her rug is dirty it is just as if she were dirty herself.

Thus by failure in understanding, each is in danger of ignoring the other's needs, and especially of not realizing their tremendous importance to the other. One may even laugh at these needs, making light of such a hobby as the husband's stamp collection or the wife's oil paintings. To make light of these is to inflict deep wounds. A joke between lovers may be full of charm, but when mockery betrays lack of understanding, it can do grave harm.

There are also the basic differences between human types: extroverts who love social life, gaiety, and movement, and introverts who seek tranquility and serious thought. C. G. Jung has described them and has also shown us that reason and sentiment are like opposite poles, as are intuition and realism. Instinctively, a very rational man is going to marry a very sentimental woman. Their complementing one another will, at the beginning, elicit an enthusiastic reaction in him. But later on he will want to make her listen to the objective arguments of reason; he will become annoyed at not being successful in this. He will try to show her that she is not logical in her sentimental explosions. This does not worry her at all. On her part, she will reproach her husband for his ice-cold rational manner which stifles all life. In the same way, an intuitive mind and a scientific mind will have great difficulty in understanding each other. For the former, things are not what they objectively are, but rather symbols of other values which he imagines and associates with them. For the latter, things are precisely what they are, nothing but that which can be measured and weighed. People so very different by nature are nevertheless made to complement each other, that through each other they may discover so much of what they've not known or sensed before. This is one of the purposes of marriage.

To Achieve Understanding,
We Must Admit How Greatly the Sexes Differ

To the differences in human types we must add those between the sexes. Man and woman are basically different, far more so than they believe. This is why they both have such great difficulty in understanding one another and such great need of one another for their growth. I will go so far as to say that never can a man completely understand a woman, nor a woman a man.

For example, man has a theoretical mind while woman has a more person-centered mind. Sometimes when I am speaking on a general matter with my wife, discussing two conflicting ideas, she will ask me right out, "Who are you talking about?" I was not speaking about anyone. I was developing an idea. Yet my wife felt the need of identifying that idea with something concrete, with some person. A woman thinks of people, and in terms of people. Take a look, for contrast's sake, at men as they gather together for a game of cards or a cup of coffee. They expound magnificent theories on the way the world should be governed and how universal peace and brotherhood can be achieved. These theories are quite abstract, detached, and unrelated to the immediate situation. If one of the wives were there, she would laugh and say, "You'd be better helping me dry the dishes or taking an interest in your son and his learning difficulties, instead of leaving me with all the worry of seeing the psychologists and teachers in order to get help for him." Thus it is from woman and under her influence that man can acquire a feeling for persons. Civilization built by men alone would remain abstract, cold, technical, and dehumanized.

A woman thinks in detail, also. Details interest her more than general ideas. She has a need to tell all the day's happenings, once she is with her husband. She has to tell which hat a friend was wearing, what kind of coat was worn by another, what the janitor or the storeclerk told her and how she replied. Soon the husband is listening very distractedly because he has not understood that his wife is so made that details are of great importance to her. To him, all this appears very small and dull. When the wife senses that her husband no longer is listening to her, that he is reading in the newspaper about the world's great problems, she feels terribly alone. And alone, she will plunge ever more deeply into details which for her ever gain in importance . . . gossip, neighborhood jealousies, and the comparison of various stores' prices.

Such a woman will become ever more talkative, telling ever more, but it will be only a monologue. As response the husband will raise his shoulders from time to time. Boredom, that greatest of all enemies to marriage, as Dr. Theodor Bovet has written, will penetrate more and more into the home. It is very clear that the man needs to learn from his wife the importance of both concrete and personal details, without which general ideas are no more than empty theory. To the degree that he comes to understand this he will be able, in turn, to broaden his wife's mental horizon, enrich her thinking, and deepen her culture. The boredom of which he will one day complain is something for which he is responsible, for it is he who should have brought deeper and more fruitful ideas to his wife.

Speech itself has a different meaning for men than it has for women. Through speech men express ideas and communicate information. Women speak in order to express feelings, emotions. This explains why a wife will relate ten times an experience she has lived. It is not to inform her husband. He cuts her off sharply, "I know it already; you've told it to me before." But she needs to tell it again in order to discharge emotional tension which the experience has built up in her heart. Many men never even get to express their feelings, to say the "I love you" that the wife would like to hear a hundred times. She asks, "Do you love me?" He replies, "You know that I do." It is not that she does not know. Rather, she would like to hear it expressed ever once more. This is the greater since her husband never says it to her.

He expresses his feelings in other ways: a caress, a look, or even a rough kind of grunt. He may, on the other hand, express his feelings in more indirect manner which his wife needs to learn to understand. I well remember one woman who was suffering from just such a lack of ever hearing a tender word from the lips of her husband. One day she came to see me quite upset. Her husband, without even having warned her, had had the workmen come to refinish her living-room floor. The whole house was upset and dirty. The furniture had to be crowded together in the hallway. This woman was most irritated. I said to her, "Each person speaks in his own way! This is how your husband tells you that he loves you. Throw your arms around him if you can understand his language. Tell him how he must love you in order to go to such expenses to give you a more beautiful living room."

Many couples live in a continuous conflict between the interests of profession and home. This is especially so when the husband's work is both interesting and challenging. Just think of our surgeon friend in New York! In a great number of homes I have noticed the same situation, not only in doctors' homes but also those of pastors, teachers, and businessmen. A wife has not understood how important to him is her husband's vocation. She married the man, not his calling. Thus, from the outset, their interests are in conflict. The man is all taken up in his work. He does not talk much about it with his wife precisely because he senses her deep irritation. His work takes him away from his wife. She sees in his work only the anxieties and problems which tire her husband and which dampen his personality when he arrives home. She sees only the business dinners to which she is not invited, the trips away from home, the overtime he has to spend at the office, the interruption of emergency phone calls. Her husband grumbles at this interruption as he puts down the telephone receiver, then airs his anger in her presence.

She does not see her husband at the patient's side, a few minutes later. She does not witness the eagerness, the care, the interest, which as a doctor he takes in the problems raised by the case.

Thus the young wife can have a strong aversion for her husband's calling, while to him it is the most thrilling thing in his life. They live in two different worlds. She puts spite into the pronunciation of the words "your office." he feels she is outside of her husband's real life, receiving only a few crumbs now and then for which she has to beg. On the other hand, she may take revenge by creating her own world around her, a world about which she talks less and less because her husband considers it as so much foolishness. Her clothes, her committees, her community groups, are to him nothing but pure vanity.

In order to understand each other, man and wife must take an interest in what interests the other, and come to understand why it interests the other. A man will talk of his interest only when he senses genuine interest in another, and it is only when he talks of it that the other can understand better the character of that interest. In this way the horizon broadens for both partners, instead of steadily narrowing. Real understanding always brings with it a going beyond one's self. Then can the home serve as a foundation to one's calling, and the calling can enrich in its turn the spiritual life of the home. The conflict from which many couples suffer can be solved. Yet, the profound differences which separate men and women are found in the very thing which brings them together: love itself.

To Achieve Understanding,
We Must Admit Our Differences in Love Itself

Once a psychologist, in comparing married life to theatre, made the following remark, "Love, for the woman, is itself the drama; for the man, it is the intermission." I think the comparison is fair. For the man, love is a very powerful impulse, greatly sexual in character, all speed and desire, and yet quickly over with. Afterward his thoughts are drawn to other matters and his wife feels that she has been forsaken. I am speaking, of course, of men who are very virile. Other men, who are interested only in love, are hardly to be so considered!

I remember a beautiful short story, whose author I cannot recall. It described a couple back home from the honeymoon. For several weeks the lovers had not been out of each other's company; they were completely each other's. And then, the next day, the husband heads back to his office. The young wife sits down on a kitchen stool and dissolves in tears, "Now, I am all alone, I am all alone!" One day, so we hope, this young wife will get up from the stool and regain an interest in life. If so, it will be because everything she will do, she will do out of love for her husband. Out of love for him she will cook, she will sweep the floor, she will wash the dishes . . . The reason for this is that love, for a woman, constitutes the whole of life.

A man, on the other hand, takes an interest in his work for the work itself, for the technical problems which have to be solved in it, for the competition in his profession, and for the attainment of success. Love, well, he will think about that when he is with his wife back at home. Even then there will be a difference: the wife has an emotional need which often the husband fails to recognize. She needs to hear tender words, she needs to go out with her husband, to share excitement with him as they admire something, to experience deep oneness with him in the silence of a moment of exaltation. For her love means a permanent, high level of affection. This is why she would like her husband always to be with her. She counts the hours he gives her, the Sundays he spends at home, the evenings he takes her out to the show. This is, for her, the way in which love is expressed. If her husband goes off to the ball game she complains, "You don't love me any more!" If he shows interest in another matter, it is because he is no longer interested in her!

Often the wife cannot experience full sexual pleasure unless the sexual experience is but a part of a larger context of mutual harmony, understanding, and a continuing communion in affection for one another. The erotic curve, in the man, takes the appearance of a rapid rise to its peak followed by an equally rapid decline. It is by nature essentially impulsive and sexual. This is why at times a wife may say, "You do not love me, you only want me!" All of which means that she can neither understand nor accept this masculine form of love, impulsive and of short duration. She would like her husband to love as she does, tenderly and continually. Such lack of un-

derstanding can lead the wife as far as to complete disgust for the sexual experience. That her husband should wish to have union with her, while they have hardly cooled off from a heated argument, this she finds quite impossible to understand.

Many wives, similarly, find it difficult to understand that a husband may be tempted sexually. That a man so prominent, so respected, so intelligent, should be in the throes of such base and vulgar temptation—at this his wife can only be completely incensed. She thinks that if he really loved her he would not think of other women, whereas it is precisely because of his love for her that he confides his struggle to her. He feels misunderstood, condemned, and despised. He withdraws into himself. Henceforth he will avoid such confidences which only cast a shadow on their marital unity. Yet, the veil of silence may well jeopardize their marriage far more than his sex drive. The best protection against sexual temptations is to be able to speak honestly of them and to find, in the wife's understanding, without any trace of complicity whatsoever, effective and affective help needed to overcome them.

We Need to Understand
in Order to Help Each Other

The matter goes much deeper. In the whole area of sex, as in many others, such as that of pride or of honesty, women are, in a general and overall fashion, more upright than men. I say "in a general and overall fashion," because nothing is more erroneous and dangerous than to make moral comparisons between human beings. We can never forget Christ's words: "But many that are first will be last, and the last first." There is no greater aberration than that of flattering oneself on one's moral virtues, or of believing oneself to be exempt of the sins which one condemns in others.

Nevertheless, speaking in the popular fashion regarding morality, I say that often the husband is less upright than the wife. Or, at the least, the man is in general more conscious of his sins than the woman is of hers. He is very conscious of his sexual lust, of his lying to his wife or to his competitor, of his cheating on income tax, or of his excessive pride in his work. Perhaps this is one reason why he goes to church less willingly than his wife. He feels less at ease there. He feels a little pharisaical in thus publicly parading his piety, for he very well knows what is not right in his real life and what he does not feel capable of setting right. Perhaps this is also a reason why in church we see men who generally are less virile, little taken up in life's struggles: civil servants, teachers, men who can more easily lead a life apparently spotless.

Like such men, women generally are less conscious of their sins. Take jealousy for example. A woman can persecute her daughter-in-law most atrociously without the least recognition that she is being driven by jealousy. She would be deeply hurt were you to tell her so. Quite the contrary, she is fully persuaded that she is acting out of love. It is out of love for her son, and also for her daughter-in-law, she thinks, that she scolds her for those shortcomings she sees, and tries to have her correct them. She wants her son and daughter-in-law to be happy! She can listen to moving sermons on love and be stirred by them in her heart without the smallest twinge of conscience. She is without any perception of the aggressiveness and hostility she bears toward her daughter-in-law, who, by the way, receives her good counsel with such bad grace! Perhaps this is one reason why there are so many women with countless scruples, seeking to discover small sins since they are oblivious of the other ones.

The result is that, generally speaking, the husband is laden with a heavier burden of real guilt-feeling. It is made so much more difficult for him to speak honestly to his wife since she seems, both to him and to herself, to be more virtuous. How could she understand him, she whose life is so much worthier. He is afraid that she may disdain him. To him she appears as a policeman, an incarnation of moral law. This may explain why he will find it harder also to speak to a pastor or a priest. In his eyes, they too are

the moral law incarnate. Thus, he may well open up
to a woman culturally and socially his inferior. She
may be a little freer, one whom he respects far less
than his wife, really, but one with whom he feels at ease.
She admires and approves of him as he is, even that
part of his behavior of which he himself is ashamed.

This is the driving force of much adultery, so se-
verely denounced by the virtuous and scandalized
wife once she discovers it. Here again she is persuaded that she is motivated by love for her husband,
but she merely puts the last bricks into the wall
which separates them. From the viewpoint of morality, this woman draped in virtue is in the right. She
has all the world as witness to her uprightness. If I
risk suggesting that she try to understand her husband, she will conclude that I am taking sides for
him and against morality.

However, it is because he failed to find understanding in his wife, and that for a long time preced-
ing, that this husband let himself go along a pathway
which even he condemns. Again his feelings of guilt
and his regressive and withdrawal reflexes are accen-
tuated. Adultery may not be, in every case, a problem
of sex. Of course, this is not usually the case; I am
not living in a dreamworld! Nevertheless, even in his
sensual temptations, as in his deviations from honesty or lack of humility, a man can be helped only if
he feels understood and accepted, as he is and with
all his misery. Such a generous acceptance is then for
him a reflection of the mercy of God. For God loves
us not for our virtues but for our need: "Those who

are well have no need of a physician, but those who are sick," said Jesus.

We need to see that universal sickness, that innumerable throng of men and women laden down with their secrets, laden down with their fears, their sufferings, their sorrows, their disappointments, and their guilt. We need to understand how tragically alone they find themselves. They may take part in social life, may even play a leading role there, chairing club meetings, winning sports championships, going to the movies with their wives. Yet what eats away at them from within is that they may live years without finding anyone in whom they have enough confidence to unburden themselves.

In Order to Understand,
We Need to Grasp the Importance of the Past

Men always feel that they are judged by their appearance. However, today's appearance is the longtime result of a chain of events going back to their early wounds. All men are themselves just as surely victims as transgressors. They may seek out a psychotherapist. They are confident that a psychotherapist will not judge them, that he will, on the contrary, seek to understand what has taken place in their lives, and why they have become what they are. Of course, for those who really are sick, psychotherapy is necessary. Such therapy is both long and difficult because with the more tragic experiences the strongest resistance is built up to any deep self-discovery. Nevertheless, psychotherapists will never be able to treat all the human emotional suffering and illness that there is. Even if they were ten times as numerous, they could not do it, no more than can the pastors and priests adequately meet this need. It is imperative, in fact, that all of us, in some fashion, become psychotherapists for one another.

The essential part of psychotherapy is listening, long and passionate listening, with love and respect and with a real effort at understanding. It is the effort to go beyond the apparent and to discover the hidden or distant causation. This is the daily experience of psychologists. They hear a man tell his life story, in a hasty manner at first, simplified and laid out something like a biographical data sheet. It is not possible yet to understand very much in such a too-schematized account. But we must not interrupt him. It is after he has said all that seemed important to him that other memories, more emotionally charged, will come to his mind. Often these are incidents of such little apparent importance that he would not have thought of telling them had he not been encouraged by the complete attention with which we listen to him.

Thus, bit by bit, he discovers the importance of these incidents. Now we can understand him because he is beginning to understand himself better. He realizes the importance of his very first childhood impressions, of the way in which he became conscious of himself and of the world around him. He recalls his first relationships with his parents, each of them, then with his brothers and sisters and with others who gradually entered into his world. Modern psychology has taught us the decisive role played by our earliest experiences. Our lifelong attitudes to others were determined by them. Many of these events we have forgotten. It is by talking about them that reminiscences come, or even dreams which present them to us in veiled symbolism.

It is thus vain to hope to understand one's husband or wife without listening long, and with great interest, to his childhood and adolescent stories. What a marvelous and prodigious adventure it is when this exploration is undertaken, when this discovery of both oneself and one's partner can be made in marriage. Then there comes to fulfillment every young couple's hope in marriage: the hope that they shall be able really to help one another. It is not only a liberating help for each, but also a quite new quality of closeness which illuminates their marriage: it is the building of a greater and more creative happiness. I lost my father when I was three months old. That is to say, I never mourned him; I was not conscious of how greatly this loss had marked my life with frustration. Well I remember the day when, after a long talk with my wife in which we really sensed the presence of God, suddenly I broke out sobbing. I got rid of an emotional charge which had been for so long a time repressed. I did not then realize, nor did she, that my wife had that day played the part of a psychotherapist. This was going to open to me just such a career.

In such an adventure, each partner in marriage develops. Each is able to go beyond the natural reflexes of his personality type and of his sex. There is a complete exchange. Each gives to the other the most precious dimension of his personality, and each gives the other that which was most missing. It is no longer a question of masculine or feminine love, but of much more deeply human love in which each particular aspect of love is integrated. Finally, there is the sense of oneness which is not realized until they are sure that they no longer have anything hidden from each other.

All this is not to say that we shall no longer have anything to discover or to say to one another. Just the opposite is so! It is not a stage which we reach, but a movement we begin and which develops continuously. Once having had the priceless experience of mutual understanding, the desire for even better understanding grows. More than that: nothing helps us to open up quite as much as sensing in our life partner the desire to understand. The couple will together go back over the events of their youthful lives. Together they will see a certain tree to which a little girl used to come every day in order to share her dearest secrets, just as if to an intimate friend. Together they will stand upon the bluff from which a young boy used to look out on the world and build up his dream world and life achievements.

Yet, there are not only beautiful memories, not only memories of pain inflicted by chance or by the misunderstanding and ill will of others. These are also all those things of which we are ashamed, all those things in our past that we should like to blot out, things for which we feel ourselves responsible.

For these matters our marital dialogue turns into a kind of confession. This is not to say that it takes the place of ritual confession for the Catholic, nor of public worship for the Protestant. Yet, though it may have lesser religious value, it may well be of greater value in other ways. It is much more difficult to bare one's sins to the very person with whom we share our life, and whose love and respect we want more than anything else. The experience may well be reciprocal, for a courageous confession often calls forth another, in response, from one's partner. Then, the tremendous joy shared is a true reflection of the grace of God experienced in the life of his church.

Complete Understanding
Calls for Personal Submission to Jesus Christ

Yes, the couple's joy is complete if they can see the real and spiritual meaning of their experience. At this point I should like to complete the story of my American colleague. If he told me about the Friday evening moviegoing, it was because later on much greater things had happened in his life. He met Jesus Christ; he received Christ as master of his life. Immediately he began to listen to his wife in a quite different spirit. Thus it is with every authentic and living Christian experience. God is passionately interested in each human being. To receive God is also, therefore, to receive his intense interest for those with whom we have rubbed shoulders without really seeing or understanding them. It is impossible to open one's heart to God without also opening it to one's fellow.

The converse is also true, since God is always seeking man so as to set him free from his loneliness and confusion. Every person who sincerely draws close to his neighbor becomes an instrument of divine love, even if one or both of them be unbelieving. My surgeon friend, however, was well aware that it was God himself who had opened his eyes and put into his heart this new passion to understand his wife.

Now it was no longer such and such a need of his wife's that he could recognize; it was his wife herself that he had begun to understand. The counsel received from his psychiatrist friend had been good, that is, to take his wife out at least once a week. This had been suggested quite tactfully and had been well received. Yet, it was essentially only advice. The surgeon followed it to the letter. Basically, however, nothing had changed in his attitude toward his wife. What was needed was an inner illumination, and such illumination is never simply an intellectual matter. It is a spiritual experience.

One day the surgeon began to feel terribly responsible for his wife's nervous condition. He knew that simply sending her to a psychiatrist would not discharge him of his responsibility. While he was leading a most thrilling life at the hospital, performing operations, saving lives, doing research, writing for medical journals . . . back at home his wife was dying of emotional starvation. And he had been blind to it all!

This is what the psychiatrist had seen, and he had given wise counsel. Psychology thus may reveal problems and suggest wise measures to be taken. But the real solution of problems demands a more profound change, one of a spiritual nature. It is this change in spirit which the Bible calls "metanoia," or "repentance": change of spirit and also self-examination, humiliation, a conscious acceptance of responsibilities hitherto ignored.

In view of the proportions which marriage conflicts have taken, we have multiplied courses on marriage preparation and the whole field of marriage counseling has developed. All this is to the good. Yet, it is quite clear that neither courses nor counseling will ever suffice in the face of our present widespread breakdown of marriage. We need more than good counsel. We need a new moral contagion, one which brings about a change in deep-seated attitudes. We need a breath of fresh air, the breath of God's Spirit. No other force in the world can touch a man more deeply in his heart and make him more apt, at last, at understanding others. He sees his responsibilities. He understands that he was hurting the person whom he did not understand. He realizes that failure to understand and unwillingness to seek understanding are what caused his withdrawal into blind self-centeredness.

One husband used to denounce his wife's faults and complain of his ill fortune in being married to her. The same man now realizes his own responsibility for those faults, since he has not been able to give her the marital climate in which she might have grown, progressed, reached fulfillment, and overcome, with his help, her personal problems. It is because she has not felt understood that she has regressed, that she has hardened in her natural defensive reactions. She was able to find understanding in a psychotherapist. However, when she finds this understanding in her husband, it becomes much more beneficial.

Such was the experience of this American couple: a living faith—no longer simply a religion of ideas or sentiment—had transformed their life. "And do you realize," the surgeon told me, "we no longer go to

the movies every Friday evening. We no longer feel the need of that. Nor do we have more time than what is really needed in order to open up to each other, in order to say all those things we never dreamt of sharing before, in order to discover and to understand each other and to seek together God's leading for our home."

You well know that beautiful prayer of Francis of Assisi: "Lord! Grant that I may seek more to understand than to be understood . . ." It is this new desire which the Holy Spirit awakens in couples and which transforms their marriage. As long as a man is preoccupied primarily with being understood by his wife, he is miserable, overcome with self-pity, the spirit of demanding, and bitter withdrawal. As soon as he becomes preoccupied with understanding her, seeking to understand that which he had not before understood, and with his own wrongdoing in not having understood her, then the direction taken by events begins to change. You know those films in which the automobile wheels seem to turn backward because of the timing of the film's frames, unseen by our eyes. Well, this same type of wheel, this same chain of events which drives the person who feels misunderstood to withdraw into himself, and thus to be ever less understood, this vicious circle can be reversed when it is seen in a new light. As soon as a person feels understood, he opens up, and because he lowers his defenses he is also able to make himself better understood.

All this seems so simple when we stop to think about it. Why, then, is such behavior so rare? The

reason is that a vital spark is needed, something which sets into motion all this change in inner attitudes. This spark, however, cannot be produced by any pat recipe. We may help someone over a long period of time, using great care, knowledge, and sensitivity. Yet, the spark may never be produced. We can be helpful to a man, provide him with self knowledge through various tests, dream analyses, and offer him good counsel. We may thus obtain some real progress and yet see no decisive inner change which might change his basic attitude in life. This becomes for him a laborious task, a kind of school in which he has to follow every step of the course of studies without any idea whether he will ever obtain the diploma. The man can understand and learn many things, but the key to understanding itself he may fail to find.

To find the key to understanding, the secret of living—this is an inner experience, a discovery, a conversion, and not simply an acquisition of new knowledge. It may happen at the very time when a person feels most disheartened; it generally takes place in a way which he could not have imagined. He may have read many books, heard many sermons, accumulated much knowledge. And yet suddenly, it is a rather insignificant happening which strikes him, a word, an encounter, a death, a recovery, a look, or a natural event. God uses such to reach a man.

Even when the psychotherapist contributes to this experience, it is almost unknown to him. It is without his having realized what was happening and without his having willed or worked for it. His contribution has had less to do with his skill than with the comprehensive love he showed the patient, and that mysterious personal relationship which linked them to each other. Thus it is a spiritual event.

Yes, every good happening is of God, a gift of God. Every deliverance from loneliness, fear, suffering, or remorse is a result of the loving mercy of God. This is so even if neither the recipient nor the instrument recognize it, and take all the credit themselves.

Happy are the couples who do recognize and understand that their happiness is a gift of God, who can kneel together to express their thanks not only for the love which he has put in their hearts, the children he has given them, or all of life's joys, but also for the progress in their marriage which he brings about through that hard school of mutual understanding.

However, it is precisely in the area of religion that men are the most fearful of showing their real feelings! Even in a very happy marriage. Often I am

amazed by it. Here is the case of a couple married in
the church, with a Christian ideal, and each of them
a pious believer. Both of them go to church and par-
take of communion. I ask them, "Do you pray together? Do you share your times of meditation?"
"No," they answer. Or only learned prayers, conven-
tional and without life, prayers recited out of duty
and not of a spontaneous nature. At the bedside of
their sick child each of them may inwardly be thinking, "We ought to pray together." Yet, neither has
the courage to suggest it. One or both of them may
tell me, "I would not dare pray out loud in my partner's presence." They may not even know how to
pray silently together.

Of course, they may discuss philosophical and religious questions, theological and ecclesiastical. But
express their innermost convictions, their own experiences, their own doubts, their own feelings, their
own relationship to God—this is quite another matter! It is the highest tie binding a couple together and
yet it is rare.

Sometimes there are unusual misunderstandings
between man and wife in this area. Here is a very
religious woman who, with the enthusiasm of her
conversion experience, no longer shows interest in
anything but religious matters, who never gets ex-
cited except when she is talking about them. She
reads only religious books, and attends all the religious meetings. Speaking of her husband, she con-
fided to me her concern: how greatly she wanted her
husband to be converted! "Think of it," she told me,
"I cannot even know if he believes in something! In

vain I ask him to come to church with me or to answer my questions. There's nothing I can do. He is completely indifferent."

One day, this husband, in turn, came to see me. Quickly, spontaneously, without my encouragement, he began to bring up religious questions which were bothering him a great deal. The interview with him on this subject was most interesting, much more so than with his wife. She had quite simply adopted a complete block of doctrine. He, on the other hand, had done a great deal of thinking. He seemed to me a deeply religious person. He had a perception of what is mystery, of shades of difference and uncertainty, and of the limitations of human knowledge which can never completely penetrate the greatness of God.

Most of all, he told me that he has the highest admiration for his wife's faith, that he admires and somewhat envies her for her boldness in proclaiming it, and in settling questions which to him are so complex. Why then does he avoid all discussion with her about religion? Maybe it is because of this difference in their temperament, because he fears that she will mistake for unbelief the slightest reservation that he might make concerning her very sure affirmations.

As a matter of fact, there are very religious people who remain distant and hidden and who are considered indifferent by their partner or their pastor. There are also couples who can pray together without really expressing to one another their ideas on the questions that faith poses for them. There is thus need for bringing faith and life together, if faith is to make a difference and if life is to be transformed. A bringing together of faith and marital life is needed, so that faith may bring its incomparable transforming power and its understanding, and so that martial life may attain its fullness.

How can the two be brought together? That depends less upon what we do than upon what we are. It is more a matter of attitude than of method. We can at any rate ask God to lead us there, to show us the way, himself to bring about this total unity which is, according to his plan, to be the experience of marriage.

Whatever one's past experiences may have been, new clouds will always appear. Just as soon, then, as our sensitive feelings are again hurt, our first instinctive reaction will always be to clam up, to withdraw, and to hide our real self. But in our silent moments in God's presence, silent moments so full of truth, love, and respect for others, a second movement of the soul can bring us to overcome this holding back of ourselves which took over so quickly and which could again jeopardize our marital oneness. Because of such moments we have come to experience much more than a wonderful marriage; we have come, through each other, to experience God himself.